Spring Har
Bible Work

1 John

Get close to the Source in being, saying and doing

Design by Ascent Creative
Printed by Halcyon

With thanks to Malcolm Duncan for his work on 1 John
in preparation for Spring Harvest 2013.

Contents

About this book

This book is written primarily for use in a group situation, but can easily be used by individuals who want to study the book of 1 John. It can be used in a variety of contexts, so it is perhaps helpful to spell out the assumptions that we have made about the groups that will use it. These can have a variety of names – homegroups, Bible study groups, cell groups – we've used group as the generic term.

- The emphasis of the studies will be on the application of the Bible. Group members will not just learn facts, but will be encouraged to think 'How does this apply to me? What change does it require of me? What incidents or situations in my life is this relevant to?'

- Groups can encourage honesty and make space for questions and doubts. The aim of the studies is not to find the 'right answer', but to help members understand the Bible by working through their questions. The Christian faith throws up paradoxes. Events in people's lives may make particular verses difficult to understand. The group should be a safe place to express these concerns.

- Groups can give opportunities for deep friendships to develop. Group members will be encouraged to talk about their experiences, feelings, questions, hopes and fears. They will be able to offer one another pastoral support and to get involved in each other's lives.

- There is a difference between being a collection of individuals who happen to meet together every Wednesday and being an effective group who bounce ideas off each other, spark inspiration and creativity, pooling their talents and resources to create solutions together: one whose whole is definitely greater than the sum of its parts. The process of working through these studies will encourage healthy group dynamics.

Space is given for you to write answers, comments, questions and thoughts. This book will not tell you what to think, but will help you discover the truth of God's word through thinking, discussing, praying and listening.

FOR GROUP MEMBERS

- You will probably get more out of the study if you spend some time during the week reading the passage and thinking about the questions. Make a note of anything you don't understand.

- Pray that God will help you to understand the passage and show you how to apply it. Pray for other members in the group too, that they will find the study helpful.

- Be willing to take part in the discussions. The leader of the group is not there as an expert with all the answers. They will want everyone to get involved and share their thoughts and opinions.

- However, don't dominate the group! If you are aware that you are saying a lot, make space for others to contribute. Be sensitive to other group members and aim to be encouraging. If you disagree with someone, say so but without putting down their contribution.

FOR INDIVIDUALS

- Although this book is written with a group in mind, it can also be easily used by individuals. You obviously won't be able to do the group activities suggested, but you can consider how you would answer the questions and write your thoughts in the space provided.

- You may find it helpful to talk to a prayer partner about what you have learnt, and ask them to pray for you as you try and apply what you are learning to your life.

- The New International Version of the text is printed in the book. If you use a different version, then read from your own Bible as well.

Introduction to 1 John

Seeing his brothers and sisters getting led astray by false teaching and losing hope, John puts pen to paper once more. Having recorded the life and teachings of Jesus in his gospel, he now writes to counter the dangerous teaching of Gnosticism – a distortion of the Christian faith that elevated knowledge and intellectual understanding and that separated spirit and matter. Gnostics believed that all matter, including bodies, was evil and that the spirit was good. John, in contrast, emphasises the flesh and blood reality of Jesus throughout his letter. Jesus was a real human who lived among us, not an abstract idea or theory. And John knows that because John knew Jesus. This Messiah was also his friend.

And for John, it is all about Jesus. His letter starts and ends with how Jesus offers us eternal life, and is full of what Jesus has done for us. John wants his readers to be secure in their identity as children of God, to be able to speak with confidence the truth about Jesus and to be able to demonstrate in practical ways the life-changing love of God.

John writes passionately and almost repetitively about the love of God. You'll read a lot about God's love over the next few weeks! But that's not because John had run out of anything else to say. He wants his fellow Christians to be absolutely convinced about the love of God, to know beyond a shadow of a doubt that they are saved by that love and then to extend that love generously and faithfully to others. For him, it's a nonsense for people to say that they love God but don't love their brothers and sisters in Christ. You can't have one without the other and there needs to be complete integrity between our words and our actions.

John didn't write this letter as a systematic text to be studied, covering different topics neatly in sequence. We'll cover every verse in the letter over the six weeks, but some of the sessions pull together different passages that have similar themes.

Session 1: It's all about Jesus

 AIM: To discover Jesus as the central subject of John's letter.

TO SET THE SCENE

Try identifying things by just using your senses; your group leader will tell you what to do.

READ THE PASSAGE TOGETHER:

1 ¹*That which was from the beginning, which we have heard, which we have seen with our eyes, which we have looked at and our hands have touched – this we proclaim concerning the Word of life.* ²*The life appeared; we have seen it and testify to it, and we proclaim to you the eternal life, which was with the Father and has appeared to us.* ³*We proclaim to you what we have seen and heard, so that you also may have fellowship with us. And our fellowship is with the Father and with his Son, Jesus Christ.* ⁴*We write this to make our joy complete.*

1 John 1:1-4

1. John starts his letter with his main subject – Jesus. What does he say gives his writing credibility or authority?

 2. This prologue of 1 John has resonance with the prologue of John's gospel. Read John 1:1-4. What similarities between the two passages can you find?

 3. John doesn't just start his letter with Jesus, he refers to him throughout. Share out these verses, all from 1 John, and look them up to see what they say about Jesus.

1:7	2:1	2:2 & 4:10
2:6	2:22 & 5:1	2:28 & 3:2
3:3	3:5	3:8
3:16	4:9 & 5:11-13	4:14
4:15 & 5:5		

My thoughts and notes....

4. Talk some more about what these verses about Jesus mean for us. What difference do they make to our lives?

5. Let's keep talking about Jesus! This opening to John's letter tells us that we see good news in Jesus, we hear good news in Jesus and we encounter good news in Jesus. Share your favourite stories from the gospels where people see, hear or encounter Jesus. How have these stories impacted you?

One of the reasons John writes this letter is to counter Gnosticism – a distortion of the Christian faith that valued knowledge above everything else. Gnostics believed that all matter, including bodies, was evil and that the spirit was good, and was superior to the body. In contrast, John emphasises the flesh and blood reality of Jesus throughout his letter. Jesus was a real human who lived among us.

 6. John had the privilege of living at the same time as Jesus and meeting him in the flesh. How might we see Jesus, hear Jesus and encounter Jesus today? Share stories from your experience.

7. Verse 3: 'Fellowship' is in danger of becoming a Christian jargon word – one that we use but we're not quite sure what it means. How do you define fellowship? What does it mean to have fellowship with the Father and the Son? What does it mean to have fellowship with each other?

 8. Every church has strengths and weaknesses. In what ways does your church 'do fellowship' well? In what ways would you like your church to become a more authentic fellowship? How could you help to make that happen?

WORSHIP

Share out the verses about Jesus that you looked up in 1 John. Take some time to pray about these, thanking Jesus that he came for that reason and praying that the implication of that would become a reality in your life, in the life of your church and in the life of your local community.

DURING THE WEEK

Make a note of ways in which you see, hear or encounter Jesus this week – not as an eyewitness, in-the-flesh experience like John had but through reading the Bible, through other Christians, in prayer, by being sensitive to God's spirit at work in the world. How can you help people who don't know Jesus to see, hear and encounter him this week?

FOR FURTHER STUDY

Read through the whole of 1 John two or three times, allowing the words to sink into your heart and mind.

There are so many books that have been written about Jesus. Ask around the group to discover personal favourites. Or take a look at *The Jesus I Never Knew* by Philip Yancey. He says about it, 'In this book I emphasize the relational and personal rather than the scholarly. Who was this man Jesus? What was he like? No one who meets Jesus ever stays the same.'

Read Krish Kandiah's book
*Back To The Source:
30 Challenges to Be, Say
And Do Life The Jesus Way*

Session 2: Be

 AIM: To explore how encountering Jesus changes who we are.

TO SET THE SCENE

Talk about family traits or traditions. Are there similarities between members of your family – immediate or extended – in terms of interests, values, appearance or passions? Is there anything that your family is known for?

READ THE PASSAGE TOGETHER:

1 [5]*This is the message we have heard from him and declare to you: God is light; in him there is no darkness at all. [6]If we claim to have fellowship with him and yet walk in the darkness, we lie and do not live out the truth. [7]But if we walk in the light, as he is in the light, we have fellowship with one another, and the blood of Jesus, his Son, purifies us from all sin.*

[8]*If we claim to be without sin, we deceive ourselves and the truth is not in us. [9]If we confess our sins, he is faithful and just and will forgive us our sins and purify us from all unrighteousness. [10]If we claim we have not sinned, we make him out to be a liar and his word is not in us.*

2 [1]*My dear children, I write this to you so that you will not sin. But if anybody does sin, we have an advocate with the Father – Jesus Christ, the Righteous One. [2]He is the atoning sacrifice for our sins, and not only for ours but also for the sins of the whole world.*

1 John 1:5-2:2

3 [1]*See what great love the Father has lavished on us, that we should be called children of God! And that is what we are! The reason the world does not know us is that it did not know him. [2]Dear friends, now we are children of God, and what we will be has not yet been made known. But we know that when Christ appears, we shall be like him, for we shall see him as he is. [3]All who have this hope in him purify themselves, just as he is pure.*

1 John 3:1-3

1. Here we see more similarities between the way John starts this letter and his gospel. In John 1:4-9 Jesus is described as light; in 1 John 1:5 John says that God is light. What does it mean to say that God is light, and Jesus is light?

 2. Read 1 John 2:5-7; what does it mean to walk in darkness? Give a (hypothetical) example of someone walking in darkness. What would they need to do to walk in the light?

3. Verse 9 says that the route to forgiveness is confession. What place does confession have in your life? When and how do you confess?

4. How do fellowship and confession overlap? Is there a place for being honest with others about our sins?

 5. How does a relationship with Jesus change our nature? What new identity do we find in Christ? Look at 1:7; 2:2; 3:1-3.

 6. Contrast this with where the world invites us to find our identity and worth. From your experience, what are the main building blocks of people's identity in the west?

> **"I am only free to love others when I can know myself as the beloved."**
>
> *Henri Nouwen*

 7. Before we can share the good news of how Jesus changes us, we need to be convinced of it ourselves. How does your new identity in Christ impact your life now and in the future? How has it changed the way you see yourself?

 8. Verse 2:2 says that Jesus transforms not just individuals but the whole world. One of the ways he does this is through us, through transformed people impacting their communities. If we were completely secure in our new identity in Christ, how might that transform our families, our churches and our communities?

WORSHIP

You will be invited to write on a luggage label the ways in which the world encourages you to understand your identity. And then on another label, you will be invited to write the new identity that Jesus offers in him. Which will you take with you and which will you leave behind?

DURING THE WEEK

Spend some time thinking about your identity in Christ, using these questions as a guide.

- Who I am – what does Scripture say about who I am in Christ? How can I more fully embrace this identity?

- Who I am not – What assumptions about identity do we need to leave behind? What are the alternative sources from which we draw our identity? How does our encounter with Jesus challenge these other sources?

- Coming to God in the stillness – How does our rhythm of prayer impact on our identity? Can we remember who we are by remembering whose we are?

- Loved to show love, blessed to be a blessing – how can we make receiving from God a source of giving to others?

FOR FURTHER STUDY

Life of the Beloved by Henri Nouwen is a wonderful explanation of how much God loves us and how that needs to be central to our identity.

Ephesians 1: 1-14 is a rich, multi-faceted description of our new identity in Christ. Spend some time drinking it in, dwelling with one verse or phrase at a time.

Session 3: Say

 AIM: To consider how we communicate the truth about Jesus.

TO SET THE SCENE

How did you come to know Jesus? What role did hearing about Jesus play, and who told you about Jesus? Share your experiences with each other.

READ THE PASSAGE TOGETHER:

2 ³We know that we have come to know him if we keep his commands. ⁴Whoever says, 'I know him,' but does not do what he commands is a liar, and the truth is not in that person. ⁵But if anyone obeys his word, love for God is truly made complete in them. This is how we know we are in him: ⁶whoever claims to live in him must live as Jesus did.

⁷Dear friends, I am not writing you a new command but an old one, which you have had since the beginning. This old command is the message you have heard. ⁸Yet I am writing you a new command; its truth is seen in him and in you, because the darkness is passing and the true light is already shining.

⁹Anyone who claims to be in the light but hates a brother or sister is still in the darkness. ¹⁰Anyone who loves their brother and sister lives in the light, and there is nothing in them to make them stumble. ¹¹But anyone who hates a brother or sister is in the darkness and walks around in the darkness. They do not know where they are going, because the darkness has blinded them.

¹² I am writing to you, dear children,
        because your sins have been forgiven on account of his name.
¹³ I am writing to you, fathers,
        because you know him who is from the beginning.
I am writing to you, young men,
        because you have overcome the evil one.

¹⁴ I write to you, dear children,
        because you know the Father.
I write to you, fathers,
        because you know him who is from the beginning.
I write to you, young men,
        because you are strong

and the word of God lives in you,
and you have overcome the evil one.

¹⁵Do not love the world or anything in the world. If anyone loves the world, love for the Father is not in them. ¹⁶For everything in the world – the lust of the flesh, the lust of the eyes, and the pride of life – comes not from the Father but from the world. ¹⁷The world and its desires pass away, but whoever does the will of God lives for ever.

¹⁸Dear children, this is the last hour; and as you have heard that the antichrist is coming, even now many antichrists have come. This is how we know it is the last hour. ¹⁹They went out from us, but they did not really belong to us. For if they had belonged to us, they would have remained with us; but their going showed that none of them belonged to us.

²⁰But you have an anointing from the Holy One, and all of you know the truth. ²¹I do not write to you because you do not know the truth, but because you do know it and because no lie comes from the truth. ²²Who is the liar? It is whoever denies that Jesus is the Christ. Such a person is the antichrist – denying the Father and the Son. ²³No one who denies the Son has the Father; whoever acknowledges the Son has the Father also.

²⁴As for you, see that what you have heard from the beginning remains in you. If it does, you also will remain in the Son and in the Father. ²⁵And this is what he promised us – eternal life.

²⁶I am writing these things to you about those who are trying to lead you astray. ²⁷As for you, the anointing you received from him remains in you, and you do not need anyone to teach you. But as his anointing teaches you about all things and as that anointing is real, not counterfeit – just as it has taught you, remain in him

1 John 2:3-27

4 ¹Dear friends, do not believe every spirit, but test the spirits to see whether they are from God, because many false prophets have gone out into the world. ²This is how you can recognise the Spirit of God: every spirit that acknowledges that Jesus Christ has come in the flesh is from God, ³but every spirit that does not acknowledge Jesus is not from God. This is the spirit of the antichrist, which you have heard is coming and even now is already in the world.

⁴You, dear children, are from God and have overcome them, because the one who is in you is greater than the one who is in the world. ⁵They are from the world and therefore speak from the viewpoint of the world, and the world listens to them. ⁶We are from God, and whoever knows God listens to us; but whoever is not from God does not listen to us. This is how we recognise the Spirit of truth and the spirit of falsehood.

1 John 4:1-6

1. Look at the verses in these passages where John says he is writing – 2:7, 2:8, 2:12, 2:13, 2:14, 2:21, 2:26. What is he writing about and why is he writing?

 2. Verse 4 highlights the need for integrity in our speech and actions – if we don't do what we say we are liars. Who do you know who puts their words into actions and what impact does this have on those around them?

 3. In this letter, John shares through the written word the way of truth for a Christian community. Talk about the different ways the truth about Jesus is shared in your church. Who can be involved in this? What role do you have to play?

 4. How do you speak the truth about Jesus to the community around you – as individuals, as families or households, as a small group, as a church? Talk honestly about your experience and feelings. What would help you to do this better?

5. Write a list of dos and don'ts for a church or small group that wants to tell their culture or community the truth about Jesus.

6. In 1 John 3:18, John says, 'Dear children, let us not love with words or tongue but with actions and in truth.' How would you respond to someone who says, 'We don't need to talk about Jesus any more; we need to demonstrate the love of Christ through what we do'?

7. In 1 John 2:15, John says 'do not love the world...' and yet in his gospel in John 3:16, John writes 'For God so loved the world...' Is John contradicting himself? What is meant by 'world' in each of those verses? How are we to behave if we want to be like God and love the 'world', but do what John says and not love the 'world'?!

The Greek word that is translated 'antichrist' is unique to 1 and 2 John. Literally, the word means 'against Christ.' John warns about an antichrist that is coming, but also says that many antichrists have already come (1 John 2:18).

An antichrist is someone who denies that Jesus is the Messiah (1 John 2:22). Some people think that towards the end of the world there will be one public figure who will be The Antichrist; some have already identified it as a particular politician or world leader.

But that isn't really the best way to understand it. Rather, John seems to be saying that anyone who denies that Jesus is the Messiah is an antichrist. That could be people in our families, communities and even churches. Verse 19 could refer to the Jews in John 6:66 who stopped following Jesus because they found his teaching too hard.

8. John talks about antichrists in 2:18-22 and 4:3. What should our attitude be to those who are anti-Christ, who are against Jesus? Should we persevere in speaking the truth or stop because they are no longer listening (1 John 4:6)?

My thoughts and notes....

WORSHIP

On a map or a sketch of your local community, mark the people, places or groups to whom you would like to communicate the truth about Jesus. Pray for each other that you would have opportunities to speak and relevantly and appropriately into these relationships and situations. How can you support one another in that?

DURING THE WEEK

Something to think and pray about: 1 Peter 3:15 says, 'Always be prepared to give an answer to everyone who asks you to give the reason for the hope that you have. But do this with gentleness and respect.' Peter assumes that there will be something in the life of a believer that will provoke someone to ask about the hope they have. What kind of questions does your life provoke?

FOR FURTHER STUDY

During 2013, the Evangelical Alliance is focusing on helping Christians to talk about their faith through their Confidence in the Gospel campaign. You can read about it and find resources on their website:

www.eauk.org/church/campaigns/confidence-in-the-gospel/

The gospel of John records some conversations that Jesus had with people where he talked about who he was and what he had come to do. What can you learn from these about communicating relevantly and appropriately the truth about who Jesus is to those you meet?

▶ Jesus meets Nicodemus: John 3:1-21

▶ Jesus meets the woman at the well: John 4:1-42

My thoughts and notes....

Session 4: Do

 AIM: To explore how we can love with actions and in truth.

TO SET THE SCENE

See if you can identify a job by someone miming a typical action.

Or talk about the actions you take as part of your everyday work or activities.

READ THE PASSAGE TOGETHER:

2 ²⁸And now, dear children, continue in him, so that when he appears we may be confident and unashamed before him at his coming.

²⁹If you know that he is righteous, you know that everyone who does what is right has been born of him.

3 ¹See what great love the Father has lavished on us, that we should be called children of God! And that is what we are! The reason the world does not know us is that it did not know him. ²Dear friends, now we are children of God, and what we will be has not yet been made known. But we know that when Christ appears, we shall be like him, for we shall see him as he is. ³All who have this hope in him purify themselves, just as he is pure.

⁴Everyone who sins breaks the law; in fact, sin is lawlessness. ⁵But you know that he appeared so that he might take away our sins. And in him is no sin. ⁶No one who lives in him keeps on sinning. No one who continues to sin has either seen him or known him.

⁷Dear children, do not let anyone lead you astray. The one who does what is right is righteous, just as he is righteous. ⁸The one who does what is sinful is of the devil, because the devil has been sinning from the beginning. The reason the Son of God appeared was to destroy the devil's work. ⁹No one who is born of God will continue to sin, because God's seed remains in them; they cannot go on sinning, because they have been born of God. ¹⁰This is how we know who the children of God are and who the children of the devil are: anyone who does not do what is right is not God's child, nor is anyone who does not love their brother and sister.

¹¹For this is the message you heard from the beginning: we should love one another.

¹²Do not be like Cain, who belonged to the evil one and murdered his brother. And why did he murder him? Because his own actions were evil and his brother's were righteous. ¹³Do not be surprised, my brothers and sisters, if the world hates you. ¹⁴We know that we have passed from death to life, because we love each other. Anyone who does not love remains in death. ¹⁵Anyone who hates a brother or sister is a murderer, and you know that no murderer has eternal life residing in him.

¹⁶This is how we know what love is: Jesus Christ laid down his life for us. And we ought to lay down our lives for our brothers and sisters. ¹⁷If anyone has material possessions and sees a brother or sister in need but has no pity on them, how can the love of God be in that person? ¹⁸Dear children, let us not love with words or speech but with actions and in truth.

¹⁹This is how we know that we belong to the truth and how we set our hearts at rest in his presence: ²⁰if our hearts condemn us, we know that God is greater than our hearts, and he knows everything. ²¹Dear friends, if our hearts do not condemn us, we have confidence before God ²²and receive from him anything we ask, because we keep his commands and do what pleases him. ²³And this is his command: to believe in the name of his Son, Jesus Christ, and to love one another as he commanded us. ²⁴The one who keeps God's commands lives in him, and he in them. And this is how we know that he lives in us: we know it by the Spirit he gave us.

1 John 2:28-3:24

1. Look through this passage and pick out the verses that talk about a believer's behaviour or actions – there are lots of them! How would you sum up John's overall message in these verses?

How does this apply to me? **2.** Read 1 John 3:1-3. How can we purify ourselves? What does this look like in practice? And why is it important?

3. John would appear to contradict himself. In 1 John 3:7-10 he says the children of God will not continue to sin. In 1 John 1:8-10 he says that if we claim we have not sinned then we are liars! How can we reconcile these two passages?

How does this apply to me? **4.** 1 John 3:18 seems a central verse for John's letter. When have you been on the receiving end of someone loving in actions and in truth? What impact did that have on you?

My thoughts and notes....

> "Genuine biblical faith in God takes us to a place that is beyond intellectual assent and a mere collation of correct ideas about God. It transforms us into carriers and transmitters of the very love that rescued us in the first place."
>
> *Alan Hirsch*
> *Right Here Right Now: Everyday Mission for Everyday People*

What about my church? **5.** In what ways does your church love in actions and in truth, both the people within it and the surrounding community? What opportunities are there for your church to put love into action? How do you discern what God is calling you to do?

6. John says that we need to love our fellow brothers and sisters in Christ - verses 3:11-15 – but we know from experience that sometimes it is hard to even like each other! How should we address disputes, disagreements and personality clashes with our fellow Christians? How could you love those in your church better?

How does this apply to me? **7.** 1 John 3:17 is very challenging – many of us have more than enough material possessions and we can't avoid seeing brothers and sisters in need. How do we choose a wise response on the scale from being overwhelmed to being hard-hearted? How do we discern what is a right standard of living in our world?

WORSHIP

Take a few moments to think on your own about how you could love in actions and in truth this week.

- Think about one thing you could do for the people that you live with.

- Think about one thing you could do for your church community.

- Think about one thing you could do for the wider community that you're part of.

My thoughts and notes....

You may not have time to do all three actions; which one will you start with?

If you're comfortable, share with others what you have decided to do. Then pray for each other that this would be a week overflowing with loving actions and truth.

DURING THE WEEK

Take some time to reflect on how true 1 John 3:18 is of you. Do you love with actions and in truth?

- Consider your own inner life – how obedient to God's commands are you? How well do your attitudes mirror those of Jesus?

- Consider your involvement in your church community – how do you demonstrate God's love to your brothers and sisters in Christ? Is your church known as a welcoming, redeeming community and how do you contribute to that?

- Consider your interaction with your wider community and culture – how do you bring light and hope to those around you? Are you known for the way that you love others?

Turn these reflections into action. What steps do you need to take?

FOR FURTHER STUDY

A Rocha's Living Lightly project is an initiative that came out of the growing desire of some Christians to be the change that they want to see in the world and a recognition that a biblical understanding for creation care has to be lived out in their everyday lives. Visit the website for tips on how to demonstrate the love of God in everyday actions.

www.arochalivinglightly.org.uk

Look through John's gospel for ways in which Jesus showed his love for people in actions and in truth, rather than just through words. Ask God to show you how you can follow his example.

Session 5: All you need is love

 AIM: To take another opportunity to focus on the love of God and how it might spur us to prophetic action

TO SET THE SCENE

Love is a central theme of so many films, songs, stories and plays. Talk about your favourite depictions of love in these art forms. Are there any that accurately show what the love of God is like?

READ THE PASSAGE TOGETHER:

4 ¹Dear friends, do not believe every spirit, but test the spirits to see whether they are from God, because many false prophets have gone out into the world. ²This is how you can recognise the Spirit of God: every spirit that acknowledges that Jesus Christ has come in the flesh is from God, ³but every spirit that does not acknowledge Jesus is not from God. This is the spirit of the antichrist, which you have heard is coming and even now is already in the world.

⁴You, dear children, are from God and have overcome them, because the one who is in you is greater than the one who is in the world. ⁵They are from the world and therefore speak from the viewpoint of the world, and the world listens to them. ⁶We are from God, and whoever knows God listens to us; but whoever is not from God does not listen to us. This is how we recognise the Spirit of truth and the spirit of falsehood.

⁷Dear friends, let us love one another, for love comes from God. Everyone who loves has been born of God and knows God. ⁸Whoever does not love does not know God, because God is love. ⁹This is how God showed his love among us: he sent his one and only Son into the world that we might live through him. ¹⁰This is love: not that we loved God, but that he loved us and sent his Son as an atoning sacrifice for our sins. ¹¹Dear friends, since God so loved us, we also ought to love one another. ¹²No one has ever seen God; but if we love one another, God lives in us and his love is made complete in us.

¹³This is how we know that we live in him and he in us: he has given us of his Spirit. ¹⁴And we have seen and testify that the Father has sent his Son to be the Saviour of the world. ¹⁵If anyone acknowledges that Jesus is the Son of God, God lives in them

and they in God. ¹⁶And so we know and rely on the love God has for us.

God is love. Whoever lives in love lives in God, and God in them. ¹⁷This is how love is made complete among us so that we will have confidence on the day of judgment: in this world we are like Jesus. ¹⁸There is no fear in love. But perfect love drives out fear, because fear has to do with punishment. The one who fears is not made perfect in love.

¹⁹We love because he first loved us. ²⁰Whoever claims to love God yet hates a brother or sister is a liar. For whoever does not love their brother and sister, whom they have seen, cannot love God, whom they have not seen. ²¹And he has given us this command: anyone who loves God must also love their brother and sister.

1 John 4:1-21

1. 1 John 4:7-21 is a reiteration of all that John has said so far about love. How would you summarise what he's saying in a tweet (140 characters or less)? Why do you think John felt the need to repeat himself?

2. The world perhaps understands love primarily as a feeling that comes and goes, as you may have identified in your discussion about films, books and songs. Read 1 Corinthians 13 together, Paul's wonderful hymn about love. How would you communicate from these verses that the love that God gives us and draws from us is far more than a feeling?

3. In 1 John 4:7 John says that everyone who loves has been born of God and knows God – which surely must be practically everyone in the world. How might this fact help our evangelism, the ways in which we share the good news of Jesus with others?

4. We've picked up on three themes in 1 John: Be, Say and Do – who we are as loved children of God, what we say about that love, and how we live out God's love – but in reality it's hard to separate them out completely. Which of these three comes most naturally to you? Which do you want to see increase in your life? How do they flow into each other?

My thoughts and notes....

5. John mentions the Spirit of God twice in this chapter in verse 2 and verse 13. What does he say is the role of the Spirit?

6. In 1 John 4:4-6, John highlights the fact that we are called to be different to the world around us. We come from God, we speak from his viewpoint and people will respond according to whether they know God or not. In what ways are we called to be distinctive to the world around us; what will that look like in practice? And in what ways do we need to share a common life?

"The challenge for us in our own time is to discern the forces against which we are called to stand. What are the issues over which it is appropriate for Christians to risk their lives today? The dilemma faced by the Chapter of St Paul's Cathedral when the Occupy movement took up residence brought these choices starkly into the light for many believers. In a standoff between the establishment and those protesting against it, where does the church stand? Where would Jesus be? This was, for many, a genuine dilemma – one that did not offer itself up to easy answers. Where else in our culture are such decisions buried? Where else might the call of the Holy Spirit to prophetic action be heard?"

Gerard Kelly
The Source, Spring Harvest 2013 Theme Guide

7. There are times when our love is not only practical but needs to become prophetic – embodying the purposes of God and pointing the world towards its future. Walter Brueggemann says that the role of the prophet is two-fold - to evoke grief and create amazement - grief for what has been lost, and amazement for the new worlds that are possible. What are the ways in which you would like to see your church being prophetic in your local community? What are the issues on which the church needs to take a stand?

WORSHIP

In Revelation 21, John has a vision of the New Jerusalem – what the city looks like when all things are made new at the return of Jesus. Write your vision of the renewed version of your town or village, when all sin and brokenness is put right. What would it look like? What would be different? What groups of people would be affected and how? Share these visions with each other, and talk and pray about how they could become a reality.

DURING THE WEEK

Take some time to think through the challenges facing you and your faith community. Building on the thinking you have done with this group over the last five weeks see if you can identify three issues in each of the following areas that are crying out for a Jesus-centred prophetic response.

- In the personal sphere – three things you may need to challenge

- In your local congregation – three things you can take on together

- Across your city or area – three things the body of Christ as a whole should engage with

- Globally – three things that the church should be known for its stance on.

Come to the next session ready to share your ideas.

FOR FURTHER STUDY

Read C S Lewis' classic book *The Four Loves* to understand more about the nature of love.

Spend time meditating on 1 Corinthians 13 or Ephesians 3:14-21, allowing yourself to soak in God's love until you are really grounded in it.

Look at campaigning websites such as www.38degrees.org.uk and www.change.org. Would you describe any of these actions as prophetic? How might Christians use one of these websites to be prophetic and fight injustice?

Session 6: Back to Jesus

 AIM: To reflect on what we have learned through these studies.

TO SET THE SCENE

Share your thoughts from the 'during the week' activity from the last session.

READ THE PASSAGE TOGETHER:

5 ¹Everyone who believes that Jesus is the Christ is born of God, and everyone who loves the father loves his child as well. ²This is how we know that we love the children of God: by loving God and carrying out his commands. ³In fact, this is love for God: to keep his commands. And his commands are not burdensome, ⁴for everyone born of God overcomes the world. This is the victory that has overcome the world, even our faith. ⁵Who is it that overcomes the world? Only the one who believes that Jesus is the Son of God.

⁶This is the one who came by water and blood – Jesus Christ. He did not come by water only, but by water and blood. And it is the Spirit who testifies, because the Spirit is the truth. ⁷For there are three that testify: ⁸the Spirit, the water and the blood; and the three are in agreement. ⁹We accept human testimony, but God's testimony is greater because it is the testimony of God, which he has given about his Son. ¹⁰Whoever believes in the Son of God accepts this testimony. Whoever does not believe God has made him out to be a liar, because they have not believed the testimony God has given about his Son. ¹¹And this is the testimony: God has given us eternal life, and this life is in his Son. ¹²Whoever has the Son has life; whoever does not have the Son of God does not have life.

¹³I write these things to you who believe in the name of the Son of God so that you may know that you have eternal life. ¹⁴This is the confidence we have in approaching God: that if we ask anything according to his will, he hears us. ¹⁵And if we know that he hears us – whatever we ask – we know that we have what we asked of him.

¹⁶If you see any brother or sister commit a sin that does not lead to death, you should pray and God will give them life. I refer to those whose sin does not lead to death. There is a sin that leads to death. I am not saying that you should pray about that. ¹⁷All wrongdoing is sin, and there is sin that does not lead to death.

¹⁸We know that anyone born of God does not continue to sin; the One who was born of God keeps them safe, and the evil one cannot harm them. ¹⁹We know that we are children of God, and that the whole world is under the control of the evil one. ²⁰We know also that the Son of God has come and has given us understanding, so that we may know him who is true. And we are in him who is true by being in his Son Jesus Christ. He is the true God and eternal life.

²¹Dear children, keep yourselves from idols.

1 John 5:1-21

John returns to the subject with which he started – Jesus.

1. In 1 John 5:3, John says that God's commands are not burdensome. Is this your experience? How would you advise someone who is finding God's commands burdensome?

2. John says that 'everyone who is born of God overcomes the world' in 1 John 5:4-5. What aspects of the world do you want to overcome? How do we do that in everyday life? And what does it mean for our future?

3. Echoing his most famous verse in John 3:16, John mentions eternal life several times in this epistle including verses 11, 13 and 20 in this passage. Eternal life can be quite an overwhelming concept. We are so used to life being limited that to think of it going on forever can be difficult. How should the fact that believers have eternal life affect the way that we live now?

My thoughts and notes....

What does John mean when he says that Jesus 'did not come by water only, but by water and blood'? This is what Nick Page says in *The Bible Book: A User's Guide*. 'The text is about Jesus' baptism and sacrifice. John is responding to the Cerinthians who taught that God 'took over' the body of Jesus at his baptism, but left before his death. In their view Jesus only came through water – that is, at his baptism – but not by blood – that is, by his death. But John affirms that it was the same Jesus who was baptised and who died. There was no trick substitution, no switch of identities. The one who was washed in the River Jordan was the same one who endured the muck and grime and nails of the cross; God who died and rose again.'

4) Over the last six weeks we have looked at being, saying and doing – how our relationship with Jesus affects who we are, what we say and what we do. John ends his epistle with three 'We know...' statements in verse 20. Write your own 'I know...' statements that reflect what God has impressed on you through these studies. Share them with the rest of the group.

There are different views of what John means when he talks about a sin that leads to death in 5:16. It may be that he is referring to what happened to Ananias and Sapphira in Acts 5 when their sin lead to their physical death, but it is not clear.

WORSHIP

Pray together as a group for the things that you have learned through these studies. Pray that you would be secure in your identity as beloved children of God. Pray that God would help you to communicate clearly and appropriately about the love of Jesus. Pray that you would be able to demonstrate the love of God in actions and in truth. And pray for any actions that you've decided to take as a group or as individuals – for wisdom, perseverance and the favour of God.

Leaders' Guide

TO HELP YOU LEAD

You may have led a group many times before or this may be your first time. Here is some advice on how to lead these studies.

- As a group leader, you don't have to be an expert or a lecturer. You are there to facilitate the learning of the group members – helping them to discover for themselves the wisdom in God's word. You should not be doing most of the talking or dishing out the answers, whatever the group expects from you!

- You do need to be aware of the group's dynamics, however. People can be quite quick to label themselves and each other in a group situation. One person might be seen as the expect, another the moaner who always has something to complain about. One person may be labelled as quiet and not expected to contribute; another person may always jump in with something to say. Be aware of the different type of individuals in the group, but don't allow the labels to stick. You may need to encourage those who find it hard to get a word in, and quieten down those who always have something to say. Talk to members between sessions to find out how they feel about the group.

- The sessions are planned to try and engage every member in active learning. Of course you cannot force anyone to take part if they don't want to, but it won't be too easy to be a spectator. Activities that ask everyone to write down a word, or talk in twos, and then report back to the group are there for a reason. They give everyone space to think and form their opinion, even if not everyone voices it out loud.

- Do adapt the sessions for your group as you feel is appropriate. Some groups may know each other very well and will be prepared to talk at a deep level. New groups may take a bit of time to get to know each other before making themselves vulnerable, but encourage members to share their lives with each other.

- You probably won't be able to tackle all the questions in each session so decide in advance which ones are most appropriate to your group and situation.

Encourage a number of replies to each question. The study is not about finding a single right answer, but about sharing experiences and thoughts in order to find out how to apply the Bible to people's lives. When brainstorming, don't be too quick to evaluate the contributions. Write everything down and then have a look to see which suggestions are worth keeping.

Similarly, encourage everyone to ask questions, voice doubts and discuss difficulties. Some parts of the Bible are difficult to understand. Sometimes the Christian faith throws up paradoxes. Painful things happen to us that make it difficult to see what God is doing. A group should be a safe place to express all of this. If discussion doesn't resolve the issue, send everyone away to pray about it between sessions, and ask your minister for advice.

Give yourself time in the week to read through the Bible passage and the questions. Read the Leaders' notes for the session, as different ways of presenting the questions are sometimes suggested. However during the session don't be too quick to come in with the answer – sometimes people need space to think.

Delegate as much as you like! The easiest activities to delegate are reading the text, and the worship sessions, but there are other ways to involve the group members. Giving people responsibility can help them own the session much more.

Pray for group members by name, that God would meet with them during the week. Pray for the group session, for a constructive and helpful time. Ask the Lord to equip you as you lead the group.

THE STRUCTURE OF EACH SESSION

Feedback: find out what people remember from the previous session, or if they have been able to act during the week on what was discussed last time.

To set the scene: an activity or question to get everyone thinking about the subject to be studied.

Bible reading: it's important actually to read the passage you are studying during the session. Ask someone to prepare this in advance or go around the group reading a verse or two each. Don't assume everyone will be happy to read out loud.

Questions and activities: adapt these as appropriate to your group. Some groups may enjoy a more activity-based approach; some may prefer just to discuss the questions. Try out some new things!

Worship: suggestions for creative worship and prayer are included, which give everyone an opportunity to respond to God, largely individually. Use these alongside singing or other group expressions of worship. Add a prayer time with opportunities to pray for group members and their families and friends.

For next week: this gives a specific task to do during the week, helping people to continue to think about or apply what they have learned.

Further study: suggestions are given for those people who want to study the themes further. These could be included in the group if you feel it's appropriate and if there is time.

WHAT YOU NEED

A list of materials that are needed is printed at the start of each session in the Leaders' Guide. In addition you will probably need:

Bibles: the main Bible passage is printed in the book so that all the members can work from the same version. It is useful to have other Bibles available, or to ask everyone to bring their own, so that other passages can be referred to.

Paper and pens: for people who need more space than is in the book!

Flip chart: it is helpful to write down people's comments during a brainstorming session, so that none of the suggestions is lost. There may not be space for a proper flip chart in the average lounge, and having one may make it feel too much like a business meeting or lecture. Try getting someone to write on a big sheet of paper on the floor or coffee table, and then stick this up on the wall with blu-tack.

GROUND RULES

How do people know what is expected of them in a group situation? Is it ever discussed, or do we just pick up clues from each other? You may find it helpful to discuss some ground rules for the group at the start of this course, even if your group has been going a long time. This also gives you an opportunity to talk about how you, as the leader, see the group. Ask everyone to think about what they want to get out of the course. How do they want the group to work? What values do they want to be part of the group's experience; honesty, respect, confidentiality? How do they want their contributions to be treated? You could ask everyone to write down three ground rules on slips of paper and put them in a bowl. Pass the bowl around the group. Each person takes out a rule and reads it, and someone collates the list. Discuss the ground rules that have been suggested and come up with a top five. This method enables everyone to contribute fairly anonymously. Alternatively, if your group are all quite vocal, have a straight discussion about it!

NB Not all questions in each session are covered, some are self-explanatory.

ICONS

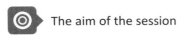 The aim of the session

 Investigate what else the Bible says

 How does this apply to me?

 What about my church?

 Engaging with the world

SESSIONS

John didn't write this letter as a systematic text to be studied, covering different topics neatly in sequence. We'll cover every verse in the letter over the six weeks, but some of the sessions pull together different passages that have similar themes.

Session 1: Notes - It's all about Jesus

YOU WILL NEED

It's helpful for each member of the group to have a Bible as well as a workbook because we'll be looking at other passages in God's word.

Items for people to identify using their senses – see **TO SET THE SCENE** for details.

Small pieces of card or blank business cards. Write a reference from question 3 on each one, ready to hand out so people can look them up.

TO SET THE SCENE

As a fun introduction, get people to identify objects just by taste, touch or sound. This links to the ways in which John encountered Jesus but also serves as an icebreaker, helping people to relax. You don't need to do all three; choose what would suit your group, being sensitive to any disabilities.

Taste – you'll need a blindfold and some items for people to taste. Try red wine (can they identify the colour?); marmite; cake and a herbal tea – or whatever is in your kitchen.

Touch – put an item in a washing up bowl covered with a cloth. Try a cauliflower; a bottle of shampoo or shower gel; a cuddly toy; a battery. How accurate can they be just using touch?

Sound – use the blindfold again. Open a can of fizzy drink; play the opening bars of a well-known tune; open and close a glasses case.

You could make the point that it's hard to be completely accurate when you're just using one sense; if you use all of them, like John's encounters with Jesus, there can be no mistaking what's in front of you.

DISCUSS TOGETHER

1. The fact that John met Jesus in the flesh – that he heard him, saw him, looked at him, touched him – gives his writing credibility. This is not just theory; John knew Jesus.

2. Both passages talk about Jesus existing from the beginning:
John 1:1 – In the beginning...
1 John 1:1 – That which was from the beginning

Both refer to Jesus as the Word:
> John 1:1 – In the beginning was the Word; verse 14 The Word became flesh
> 1 John 1:1 – this we proclaim concerning the Word of life

Both say that Jesus was with God, the Father
> John 1:1-2 – the Word was with God; He was with God in the beginning
> 1 John 1:2 – which was with the Father and has appeared to us

Both talk about the incarnation - Jesus coming in the flesh, as a human
> John 1:14 – the Word became flesh and made his dwelling among us
> 1 John 1:1 – John has seen, heard and touched Jesus.

3. Share out the cards among people, getting them to work in pairs if you like, so that each person or pair has a few references to look up. Ask people to write what that verse says about Jesus on the card to use later in the session.

1:7	Jesus purifies us from all sin
2:1	Jesus advocates to the Father for us (speaks on our behalf)
2:2 and 4:10	Jesus is the atoning sacrifice for our sins (makes us right with God by taking our sin on himself)
2.6	Jesus is our model for how to live
2:22 and 5:1	Jesus is the Messiah, the longed-for Saviour
2:28 and 3:2	Jesus will appear again; he will return
3:3	Jesus is pure
3:5	Jesus is sinless and takes away our sin
3:8	Jesus came to destroy the devil's work
3:16	Jesus laid down his life for us
4:9 and 5:11-13	Jesus gives us eternal life
4:14	Jesus is the Saviour of the world
4:15 and 5:5	Jesus is the Son of God

4. Encourage people to see how these aspects of Jesus life and mission have an impact on us. For example, Jesus purifies us from all sin which means that we can be forgiven, we can be restored to relationship with God and we can be free from the eternal consequences of what we have done.

5. Be ready to share some examples of your own.

6. We can see Jesus through the actions and example of other Christians. We can hear Jesus through God's word and by spending time in prayer. We can encounter Jesus through the love and actions of fellow believers.

7. In the New Testament, the Greek word 'fellowship' means something like 'sharing a common life', implying a close relationship of mutual commitment. Fellowship is not artificial small talk or joining a club. It's living, breathing, laughing, crying, struggling, celebrating – and all shades of experience in between – in common with other people. It is lives intertwined; it is hopes and dreams and disappointments shared; it is being real and unafraid.

8. Steer people away from whinging about the church. Encourage them to think about how they as individuals or as part of this group could help to strengthen the fellowship of your church.

WORSHIP

Use the cards from question 3. Spread them out on the floor or on a table in the middle of the group so no one feels under pressure to pray. Encourage people to take home some of the cards and meditate on that verse during the week.

Session 2: Notes - Be

YOU WILL NEED

- It's helpful for each member of the group to have a Bible as well as a workbook.

- Two luggage labels for each person plus pens; a bowl or waste-paper bin.

- Background music for worship activity (optional)

TO SET THE SCENE

This helps group members get to know each other better but also provides a good connection when talking about us being children of God. What interests, value and passions do we share with our heavenly father?

DISCUSS TOGETHER

1. This might seem a rather philosophical question but encouraging people to spell out what a statement like 'God is light' means helps to ground it in reality rather than nice theory. Some thoughts: When it's light you can see what's there and get things into perspective. God shows up what is real; there's nowhere to hide. Jesus shone light into people's lives and helped them face the truth about themselves – for example, the woman at the well.

2. Someone walking in darkness might not know where they're going, might stumble and fall, might not want their true actions, motives or even selves to be seen. For example, someone having an affair and being unfaithful to their spouse could be said to be walking in darkness. They are deceiving the person they are married to, may well be lying to cover their actions, has broken the promises they made when they got married. To come into the light they need to be honest with themselves and the other people involved about what they are doing and face the consequences of their actions.

3. Different traditions within the church will have different practices. Make space for diversity in people's responses.

4. Some people choose to make themselves accountable to a good friend or spiritual director about their weaknesses and sins. Encourage people to share their experiences without feeling they have to go into details of what they confess!

5. 1 John 1:7 says that we are purified from all sin; 2:2 says that Jesus has paid the price for our sins and for the sins of the world. 3:1-3 says that we are children of God – part of God's family. You could link back here to the activity at the start of the session.

6. These are some of the ways we are invited to find our identity and worth: through our jobs, our status and our pay packet; through our relationships – as a mother, for example; through our appearance, particularly for women, and how closely we fit the ideal; through our possessions or interests.

7. Encourage people to think about whether their identity in Christ is something they just know about in their head, or something that is genuinely part of who they are and has moved to their heart or gut.

8. We'll be thinking about this more over the next few sessions, about how our actions and words can impact others as well as our identity. For today, encourage people to think about how their be-ing – who they are – can transform their families as communities as well as what they might say or do.

WORSHIP

Give everyone two luggage labels. You might like to provide some background music for this activity. Encourage people to write on one label, all the ways in which they are tempted to base their identity on the things of this world. Give some time for people to reflect and do this. Then invite them to write on the other label the new identity that Jesus offers us, using words from this week's passages as well as other parts of the Bible. Again, give time and space to do this. Invite people to pray about their identity in Christ – thanking God for the change he has brought about in them and that that would become more of a reality. Invite people to throw away the worldly label in the bowl or bin, either during the prayers or as they leave, as a way of saying that they want to be more secure in their identity in Christ.

DURING THE WEEK

These questions were written by Gerard Kelly for the Spring Harvest Theme Guide 2013.

Session 3: Notes - Say

YOU WILL NEED

- It's helpful for each member of the group to have a Bible as well as a workbook.

- A map of the local area, or a large sheet of paper and pens

TO SET THE SCENE

It's easy to tell other Christians about how we encountered Jesus and put our faith in him because we share a common language, and a common set of beliefs and values. How comfortable do people feel sharing these same stories with those who are not yet Christians? How could they grow in confidence?

DISCUSS TOGETHER

1. John wants to communicate the truth about Jesus, to counteract the distortions of the gospel that are being spread through false teaching such as Gnosticism. He writes to remind people of the truth of what they already know and have heard about Jesus. He writes to encourage them to persevere.

2. Encourage people to share stories.

3. There will be formal teaching opportunities through sermons, bible studies or discipleship events. It's appropriate that those who lead these have knowledge and experience to share. But there are also opportunities to exhort and encourage each other to stay true to Jesus. All of us can be involved in this. Some people will have an opportunity to share the truth about Jesus with children or young people in the church through helping with youth groups, Sunday school, clubs or mentoring.

4. Often talk about personal evangelism strikes fear into the hearts of many Christians! We know we should do it but we find it difficult. Encourage people to share their struggles and opportunities. How can the group support each other? Can those who find this comes naturally share tips or encouragement?

5. This will help people to articulate and summarise the conversation from the previous question.

6. In truth we need both – the ability to talk about Jesus, and the ability to demonstrate the love of Jesus. Perhaps each of us will have our own preference; we need to be encouraged to do the other as well.

7. In John 3:16, the word for 'world' is cosmos – the whole created order of the universe. God loves everything that he has made, including people and longs to see it restored to the way God intended it to be. In 1 John 2:15 John is referring to the philosophies and systems of the world that are against God, rather as Jesus did in John 8:23.

8. We need to persevere in loving those who are against Jesus and in praying for them. We mustn't write off anyone as a hopeless case, but rather keep praying for God's spirit to be at work in their hearts. It might be appropriate to stop talking about Jesus if that antagonises them or causes them to harden their hearts.

WORSHIP

Use a map of the local area, or on a large sheet of paper make your own by drawing key local landmarks. If your group is very scattered geographically, then change the scale of your map to cover a wider area or simply use a blank sheet of paper for people to write on. This exercise may help people to identify common interests or groups.

Session 4: Notes - Do

If appropriate to your denomination, it would be very fitting to celebrate communion together at the end of this session, sharing the bread that Jesus describes as his body broken for us.

YOU WILL NEED

- It's helpful for each member of the group to have a Bible as well as a workbook.

- Slips of paper with jobs written on

- Large sheet of paper and pens

- Background music for the worship (optional)

TO SET THE SCENE

If your group likes being dramatic, write on pieces of paper the names of jobs such as police officer, full-time parent, teacher, checkout assistant, car wash attendant, hairdresser, chef and author. Get people to pick a piece of paper and then think of a typical action that person would often perform. For example, a teacher might mark lots of books so an action would be putting ticks on paper. They then mime that action to the rest of the group and see if they can guess the job.

Or get people to think about the work or activities that take up most of their week. They could mime a common action to the rest of the group and see if others can guess what they are doing.

Or just talk about the frequent actions that people do during their day-to-day work. Link this to the discussion about demonstrating the love of God through our actions.

DISCUSS TOGETHER

1. Use a large sheet of paper, for example from a flip chart, and write down the verses as people identify them. Seeing them written down will show just how many they are.

> 2:29 – people born of God do what is righteous
>
> 3:3 – we need to purify ourselves
>
> 3:6 – no one who lives in God continues sinning

3:7 – the one who does what is right is righteous

3:9 – those born of God will not continue to sin

3:10 – those who do not do what is right are not God's children

3:11 – love one another

3:16 – lay down our lives for each other

3:18 – love with actions and truth

3:22 – keep his commands and do what pleases him

3:23 – love one another

3:24 – keep his commands

2. We can purifying ourselves by confessing our sin; by avoiding the situations, people or temptations that lead us into wrong behaviours; and by receiving God's forgiveness, even if we don't feel it (1 John 3:19-20). It's important because God calls us to be like Jesus and to live in the light.

3. To highlight the contrast between these verses, ask someone to read out 1 John 3:4-10 and someone else to read 1 John 1:8-10. It's helpful to think about the context of each of these passages. In 1 John 1, John is talking about the need to walk in the light, to be honest about ourselves and our actions. In 1 John 3, he is talking about our new nature and status as children of God and how we need to live in that reality. I think the key to reconciling this seeming contrast is to understand that John is talking about the intention of our actions. Children of God should not deliberately sin; we need to be obedient and choose to do right because we belong to God. But if we do sin unintentionally, then we need to be quick to confess and to bring it into the light.

4. Encourage people to share stories.

5. Again, encourage people to speak positively about the church and about the potential there is to serve its members and the local community. Sometimes the needs of people can be overwhelming and it is important to discern what God is calling you to do, through prayer and through finding like-minded people in the church who can work together.

6. We need discernment to know when we need to 'agree to disagree' and when we should address issues. It can help to bring in a godly mediator who can help people to listen to each other. We need to let go of pride and the need to be right and learn to humbly serve each other. And disagreements and disputes should always be bathed in lots of prayer, asking God to show us where our attitudes and actions are wrong and asking his spirit to be at work in our hearts.

7. This is a difficult question but one that Christians need to discuss. It can really help to have some close friends to discuss this with, and a commitment to working it out together. We need to resist the temptation to measure ourselves against the affluent and particularly against what advertisers try to tell us we need.

WORSHIP

It may help to play some background music while people reflect. People will feel differently about sharing the actions they thought of. Some will welcome the opportunity to give voice to their thoughts and the gentle accountability that this will create. Others will want to keep their actions private. Respect these differences giving space for people to share but not applying pressure.

Session 5: Notes - All you need is love

YOU WILL NEED

- It's helpful for each member of the group to have a Bible as well as a workbook.

- Background music for the worship (optional)

TO SET THE SCENE

Encourage everyone to contribute. This activity might produce suggestions of films you could watch together as a group! Sally Hitchiner, Chaplain at Brunel University, has this to say about the film of Les Miserables: 'Les Miserables was possibly the most honest depiction of the heart of the Christian message that I've ever seen in a film. I glanced around the cinema to see everyone in hushed awe, tears in their eyes as we saw a dramatic religious conversion, heard heartfelt prayers and faith-inspired acts of grace (in contrast with moralistic, compassionless right and wrong). At the end there was a ripple of applause as people didn't know what else to do with such a beautiful story. It made me think about how many people there are out there who might find the grace of the Christian message strikes an immediate chord with them, if we were better at conveying it.'

DISCUSS TOGETHER

1. If your group are not the tweeting kind, suggest they think of a text message or even a telegram where more words cost more money. Encourage them to think about where love starts, how love is spread. John's letter would have been carefully crafted; his repetition is not a mistake. He wants people to grasp the strength of God's love for us and the importance of showing that love to others.

2. Think about love as an attitude, love as actions, love as a decision.

3. Ecclesiastes 3:11 says that God has set eternity in the human heart. Romans 1:20 says that God's invisible qualities are clearly seen in what he has made. Perhaps we need to look for connections that people already have with God, even if they don't recognise them, rather than expecting that God will be completely alien to them.

4. Encourage people to share their experience.

5. The Spirit enables people to acknowledge that Jesus is the Messiah. The Spirit lives in us as a sign that we belong to God.

6. As people talk about the need to be distinctive, remind them of the need to be loving and to love others as God loves us. Of course there is a need for tough love sometimes, but too often Christians are known for being judgemental.

7. Encourage people to think about those most in need in your community and those who do not have a voice. How can the church stand up for justice on their behalf.

WORSHIP

People could start with Revelation 21:1-2, replacing 'Jerusalem' with the name of their own town or village. Again, background music might suit some groups while they do this activity. People's visions will have different emphases according to their own interests or gifts, and it is interesting to see where there are overlapping concerns. Is there a way in which people could work together in this area?

Session 6: Notes - Back to Jesus

YOU WILL NEED

▶ It's helpful for each member of the group to have a Bible as well as a workbook.

▶ Large sheet of paper, post-its and pens (optional)

TO SET THE SCENE

Encourage people to share their thoughts. This section could take up most of the evening if people are full of ideas and energy, and particularly if people have had similar thoughts or want to tackle the same issues. Feel free to abandon the rest of the study and to spend time talking and praying about how the group can put these thoughts into action and how they can support one another. You can pick up on this section during the worship.

DISCUSS TOGETHER

1. Jesus criticised the Pharisees for turning God's commands into heavy burdens in Matthew 23. If we find God's commands burdensome, then we need to look to see if we have understood them correctly. We need to be secure in our identity as loved children of God, not needing to earn his favour. We need to choose to obey out of love not fear.

2. God wants us to be free from addictions and able to resist temptation. He wants us to discern where what the world is saying is different to his commands (1 John 4: 5). We need to make daily choices to live in God's ways, be quick to ask for forgiveness when we fail, and support one another. We also look forward to a future when Jesus returns when all sin and sickness will be wiped out, and we will live with God.

3. In the Lord's Prayer that Jesus taught his followers, we pray for God's will to be done on earth as it is in heaven. Enjoying eternal life now is about seeing God's will being done, bringing the future promise of God's kingdom into our daily reality.

4. Give people space to write and then the opportunity to share. You could give people post-it notes to write on, so that you can stick their contributions up for all to see, or collate them on a large sheet of paper.

WORSHIP

During this time of prayer, focus on either the results of the 'set the scene' activity or the responses to question 4, depending on how your group has responded.

OTHER TITLES IN THE SPRING HARVEST BIBLE STUDIES SERIES:

Acts – Building A People Of Faith
Based on the timeless book of Acts, this will help you uncover the truth of God's word and apply it to your own life.
SHB1327B

Daniel – Faith Under Fire
Daniel's faith was literally tested by fire, but his God – and our God – proves himself faithful in the most extreme of situations.
SHB1351B

David – After God's Heart
This workbook explores David's overwhelming desire for intimacy with God, and shows how we can also be those 'after God's own heart'.
SHB1324B

Exodus – Mission Of God
This workbook shows how mission is God's big idea, and challenges Christians to get involved in what God is doing.
SHB1356B

Grace – God's Amazing Gift
Looking at grace through the life of Gideon and parts of the New Testament, this workbook will help you uncover the truth of God's grace and apply it to your own life.
SHB1314B

John – Jesus At The Centre
Discover more about Jesus by looking at some of the key passages from John's gospel – inspire yourself and others to put faith into action.
SHB1329B

Matthew – Sermon On The Mount
Covering the whole of Matthew 5-7, this workbook provides the perfect introduction to the Sermon On The Mount and its radical challenges.
SHB1317B

Passion – Finding An Unshakeable Hope
Exploring the significance of the cross and resurrection for our lives, hopes and relationships will help us grow in confidence and in the character and grace of God.
SHB1319B

Psalms – Cries From The Heart
A study on 8 Psalms designed to help your small group express their heart to God while seeking God's heart for them.
SHB1315B

Ruth – Love, Honour And Obey
Ruth put her mother-in-law's needs before her own and God honoured her decision in ways she could never have imagined.
SHB1320B

Worship – One True King
The life of Daniel shows us that worship is about offering our whole lives to God.
SHB1326B

Yahweh – God In All His Fullness
7 studies which seek to guide you into a deeper grasp of the magnificence of God.
SHB1389B

Malachi – Wholehearted
6 sessions that help the reader to engage with the text and how it applies to them and their Church.
SHB1639B

Ephesians - United
6 sessions that reflect on the church and living a Christ-inspired lifestyle.
SHB1739B